RECYCLING CENTER

PIANO TUNER

AIR CONDITIONING

computer sales

computer sales

computer sales

BUTCHER

BUTCHER

BUTCHER

ART Supplies

ART Supplies

ART Supplies

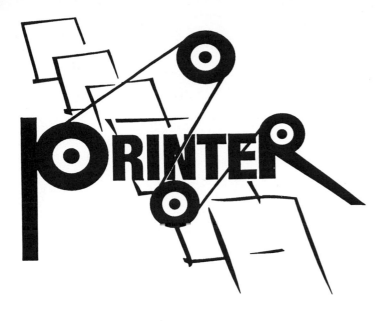

3

4

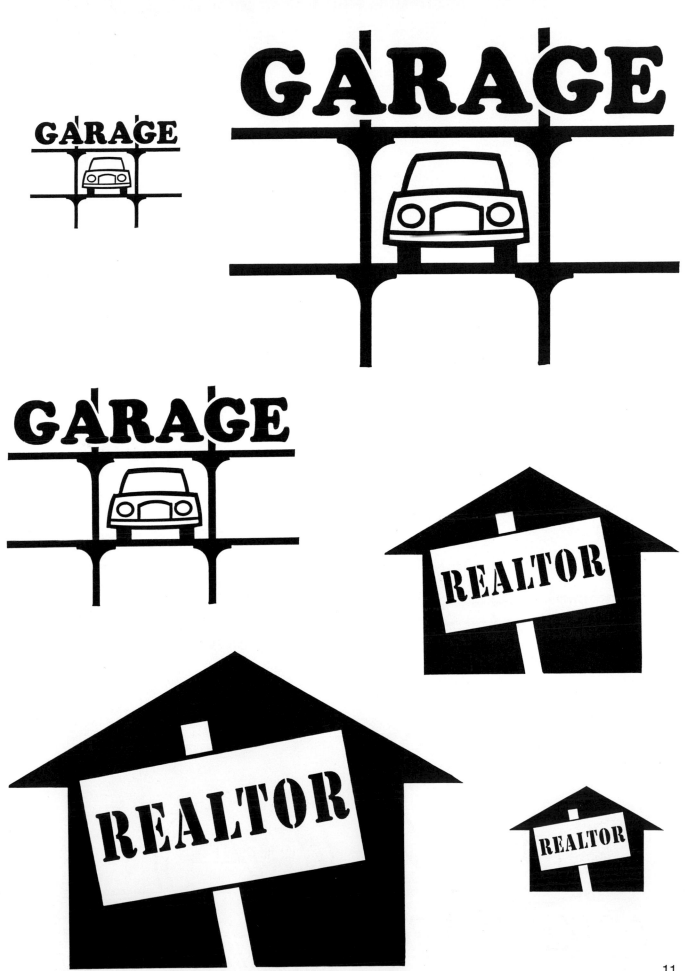

MEDICAL SUPPLIES

CAR SERVICE

CAR SERVICE

MEDICAL SUPPLIES

CAR SERVICE

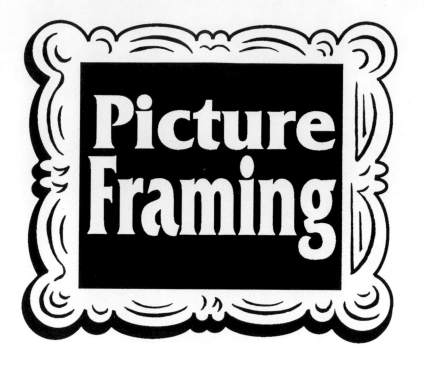

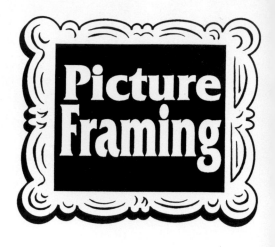

MESSENGER

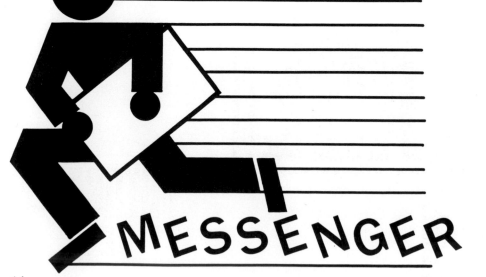

MESSENGER

MESSENGER

REPAIRS

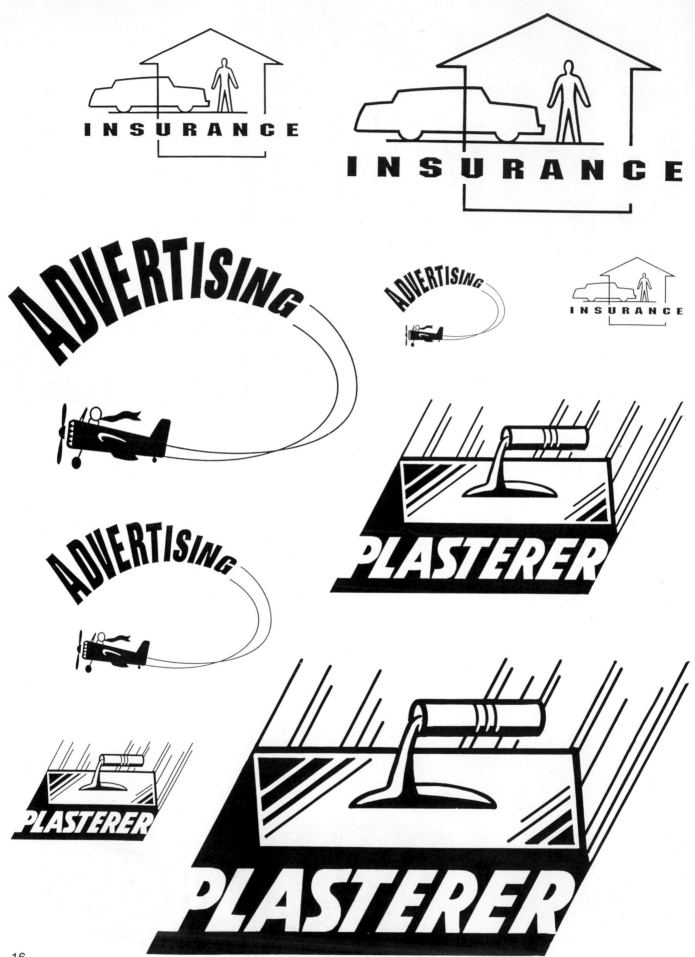

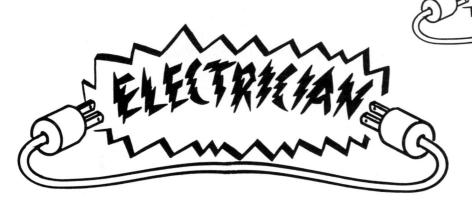

Exterminator

Exterminator

Fine
FURRIER

Fine
FURRIER

Fine
FURRIER

Exterminat--r

MUSICIANS

MUSICIANS

MUSICIANS

LIBRARIAN

LIBRARIAN

LIBRARIAN

AUTOMOBILE
REPAIR

AUTOMOBILE
REPAIR

AUTOMOBILE
REPAIR

MACHINIST

MACHINIST

MACHINIST

MEN'S CLOTHING

MEN'S CLOTHING

MEN'S CLOTHING